SSF

W9-AVC-547

The Moon & Riddles Diner and the Sunnyside Café

Nancy Willard

ILLUSTRATED BY
Chris Butler

Harcourt, Inc.

San Diego   New York   London

To Michele Burgess and Bill Kelly
—N. W.

To all my family in Idaho,
especially my father, who encouraged me as an artist;
and to Krista and Kassi, for just loving me
—C. B.

Text copyright © 2001 by Nancy Willard
Illustrations copyright © 2001 by Chris Butler

"It's Sweet Potato Day at the Sunnyside Café" was inspired by John F. H. Claiborne's
"A Trip through the Piney Woods," in *Mississippi Historical Society Publications* in 1906.
Mr. Claiborne's story was later recounted by Frank Lawrence Owsley
in *Plain Folk of the Old South*, Louisiana State University Press, 1949.

"The Spoon Boy Calls His Family for Dinner" was inspired by the article "Scientists
Stunned by Amazing Spoon Boy," *The Onion* (Madison, Wis.), 7–13, September 1993.

www.harcourt.com

Library of Congress Cataloging-in-Publication Data
Willard, Nancy.
The Moon and Riddles Diner and the Sunnyside Café/Nancy Willard; illustrated by Chris Butler.
p.   cm.
Summary: A lighthearted collection of poems about Shoofly Sally
and her Everything Dog, who meet an unusual cast of characters at an
odd restaurant called the Moon & Riddles Diner and the Sunnyside Café.
1. Restaurants—Juvenile poetry.   2. Children's poetry, American.
[1. Restaurants—Poetry.   2. American poetry.]   I. Butler, Chris, ill.   II. Title.
PS3573.I444M66   2001
811'.54—dc21   99-50834
ISBN 0-15-201941-3

First edition
A C E G H F D B

Printed in Hong Kong

The illustrations in this book are paper sculptures created with Strathmore bristol board,
enamel paint, and Elmer's glue, then backlit and photographed on Fuji film.
The display type was set in Blackfriar.
The text type was set in Cochin.
Printed by South China Printing Company, Ltd., Hong Kong
This book was printed on totally chlorine-free Nymolla Matte Art paper.
Production supervision by Sandra Grebenar and Ginger Boyer
Designed by Lydia D'moch

Photographer: Bill Ervin
Art consultant: Kassi Butler
Chef: Joanne Burlingame

The only thing I remember about our neighbor Mr. Scott is the day he moved. He had a shed full of junk and a Dumpster, and he was throwing everything away. Old magazines, newspapers. I went over to watch.

He handed me a box of postcards.

"Take 'em," he said. "Everything has to go."

I flipped through the bunch. Mostly they showed downtown buildings in places I didn't know. I thought I should choose something, so as not to hurt his feelings, and I pulled two from the pack.

The first was a picture of the First National Bank in Centersville, New York. The second showed a restaurant. At the lunch counter, a spoon and a teapot were reading the menu. Behind the counter, a frog and a bear and a buffalo were cooking pancakes on a vast stove. The caption at the bottom read:

Home on the range
at the Moon & Riddles Diner and the Sunnyside Café.

My heart jumped. I would have traded my entire allowance for a year to go there.

On the other side was a brief message:

Dear Mom and Dad,
 Don't worry about me. Great food. Good music.
I have seen the deer and heard the antelope play.
 Love,
 Shoofly Sally

I still can't read the postmark. In the morning, it looks like Rey River. In the evening, it looks like Twangsville. In between, it looks like a smear of catsup.

If you ever find the place, let me know. You'll recognize it right away from the picture. Those who aren't eating are cooking. Those who aren't cooking are hooting and hollering.

Everybody is dancing.

Sally go round the sun,
Sally go round the moon,
Sally go round the chimney-pots
On a Saturday afternoon.

—Mother Goose

Shoofly Sally
and Her Everything Dog
Take Their Show on the Road

My name is Shoofly Sally, sir.
I've traveled far and wide,
my box of biscuits on my back,
my hound dog at my side.
My shoofly pie is much admired
from Fairbanks to Bombay.
I learned to bake from a talking cake
at the Sunnyside Café.

It's there the gypsy pancakes shout
when the chicken sucks its thumb.
The kettles sneeze, the teaspoons tease
the soporific sun
till it falls asleep in a field of sheep
and the Great Bear starts to roar,
"Let the Moon & Riddles Diner, sir,
throw wide its silver door!"

It's there the hoppelpoppels dance
and the emerald antelopes sing.
My dog's as welcome as myself.
His name is Everything.
Conductors ask us where we're bound
and wait for me to say,
"The Moon & Riddles Diner, sir,
and the Sunnyside Café."

The train I took to Buffalo
was twenty hours late.
When the Buffalo King began to sing,
his voice was a squeaky gate.
He asked me, when I rose to go,
"Will nothing make you stay?"
"The Moon & Riddles Diner, sir,
and the Sunnyside Café."

The train I caught to Kankakee
got stuck in Belchertown.
I gave my heart to a gap-toothed boy
who hoped I'd settle down.
He asked me why the wild geese fly
five hundred miles a day.
"The Moon & Riddles Diner, sir,
and the Sunnyside Café."

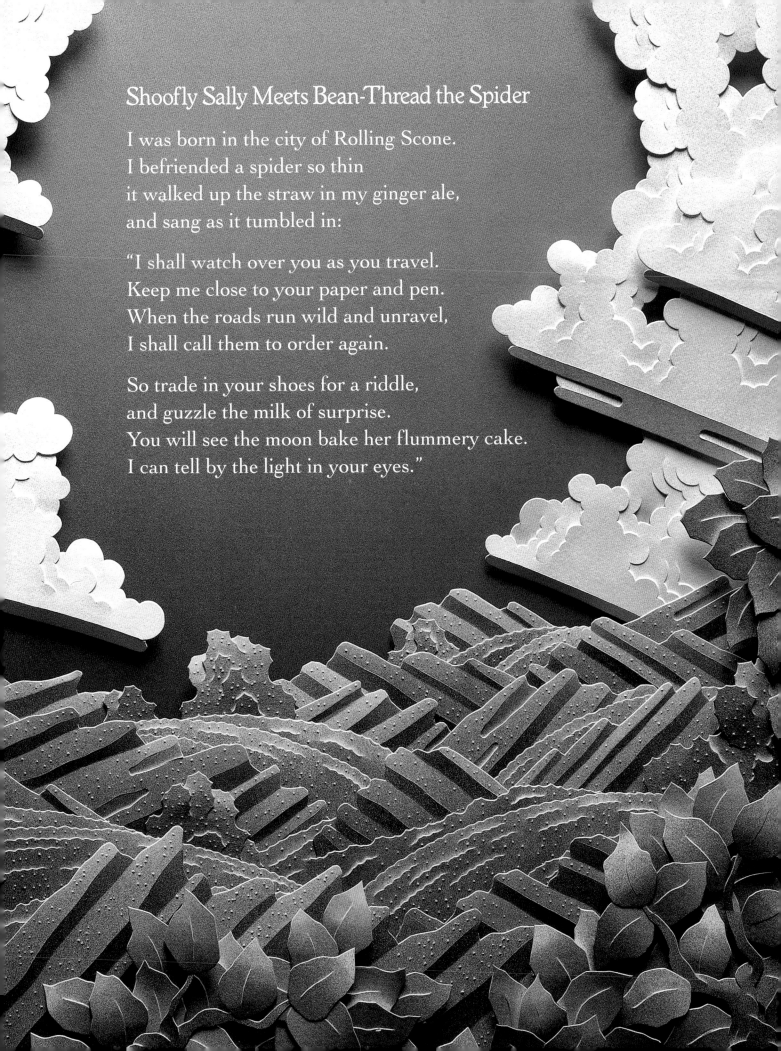

Shoofly Sally Meets Bean-Thread the Spider

I was born in the city of Rolling Scone.
I befriended a spider so thin
it walked up the straw in my ginger ale,
and sang as it tumbled in:

"I shall watch over you as you travel.
Keep me close to your paper and pen.
When the roads run wild and unravel,
I shall call them to order again.

So trade in your shoes for a riddle,
and guzzle the milk of surprise.
You will see the moon bake her flummery cake.
I can tell by the light in your eyes."

The Great Bear Goes for a Midnight Shuffle

The Moon & Riddles Diner?
It's half a smile away.
The snow-and-rain deer gather
where the emerald antelopes play

their saxophones by starlight.
They clap for the hooting moon
when the groakabies choose
to drop their shoes
in the lap of the silver spoon.

You'll hear the teapot crooning,
in a voice like the morning fog,
"The Ballad of the Riddling Ghost
and the Chuggamonga Frog."

The specialty on starry nights
is sweet tornado brew.
It comes with woodchip chile chips
and sneaky sneaker stew.

I've dined at the Woolly Bully
and the Flying Fish Café.
At the Ruby Owl
I started to howl—
when they thought I couldn't pay.

I got thrown out of the Chocolate Trout
for teaching the clams to bite.
But I love the fiddles
at the Moon & Riddles,
where they let me dance all night.

The Pample Moose Tells of His Escape

"Bring me a lasso!
Bring me a noose!
I've lost my valuable
pample moose.
The pride of my herd,
the joy of my flock,
whose stall I chained
with a golden lock."

"Giddyap," cried the moon.

I jumped through a crack.
Tell my master
I'm never coming back.

The Teapot Pours Out Her Story

My lady dropped me *crash!* on the kitchen floor.
My lady dropped me *crash!* on the kitchen floor.
She said, "Well, I got no use for this old thing anymore.

A cracked teapot is worthless as a broken fan.
A cracked teapot is worthless as a broken fan."
That lady picked me up and threw me in the garbage can.

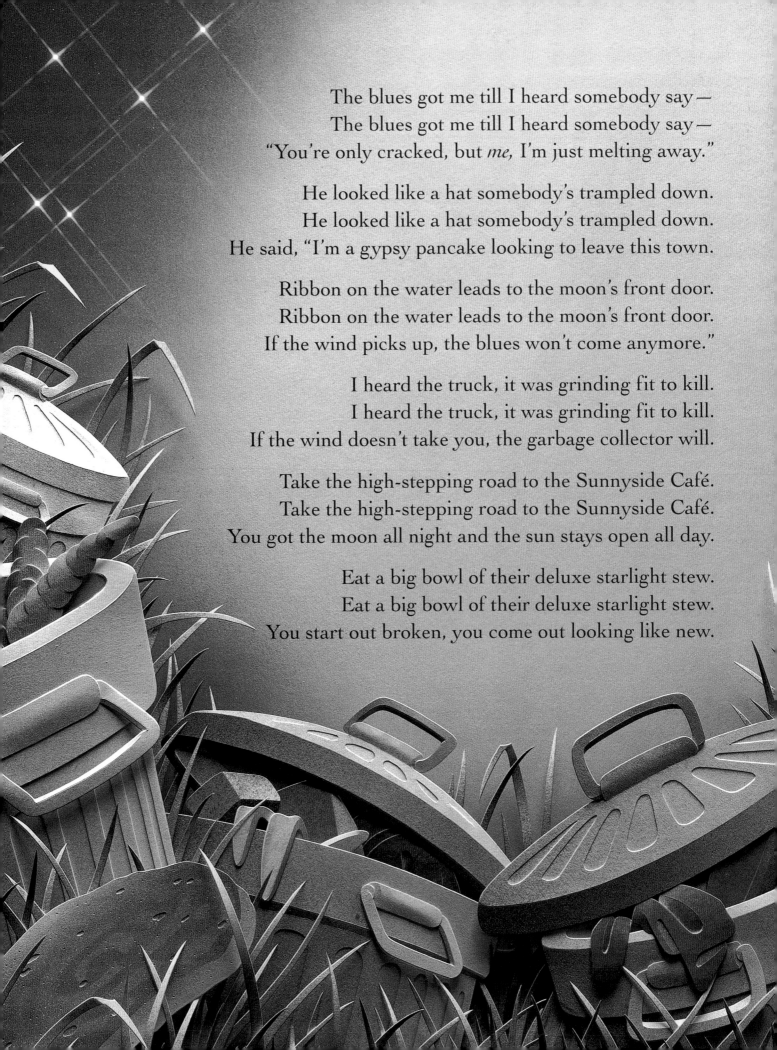

The blues got me till I heard somebody say—
The blues got me till I heard somebody say—
"You're only cracked, but *me*, I'm just melting away."

He looked like a hat somebody's trampled down.
He looked like a hat somebody's trampled down.
He said, "I'm a gypsy pancake looking to leave this town.

Ribbon on the water leads to the moon's front door.
Ribbon on the water leads to the moon's front door.
If the wind picks up, the blues won't come anymore."

I heard the truck, it was grinding fit to kill.
I heard the truck, it was grinding fit to kill.
If the wind doesn't take you, the garbage collector will.

Take the high-stepping road to the Sunnyside Café.
Take the high-stepping road to the Sunnyside Café.
You got the moon all night and the sun stays open all day.

Eat a big bowl of their deluxe starlight stew.
Eat a big bowl of their deluxe starlight stew.
You start out broken, you come out looking like new.

The Queen of Chickens Surprises a Fox

Foxy said to Her Highness for fun,
"Wings are excellent smothered in crumbs,
baked and served piping hot."
She replied, "Mine are not
wings at all. I am twiddling my thumbs."

The Moon's Report on the Stubborn Stove

Our stove has become very strange.
He cannot abide any change.
When I make the French toast
it smells strongly of roast,
and the burners play "Home on the Range."

The Ballad of the Riddling Ghost and the Chuggamonga Frog

There lived a Chuggamonga Frog
as brown as buttered toast.
She swam away from swamp and pond
to conquer the Riddling Ghost.

O riddle diddle pie

"Turn back, turn back," her mother croaked.
"You think you'll be the winner?
Suppose you fail? Suppose you wail?
He'll have your legs for dinner."

O riddle diddle pie

"He'll not eat me," boasted the frog.
"I've heard his sight is poor.
He'll think I'm on the windowsill
when I'm hiding behind the door."

O riddle diddle pie

She passed Starvation Junction
and sped through Dead Man's Jaws,
and there she spied the Riddling Ghost,
with a cleaver between his claws.

O riddle diddle pie

"Greetings, Chuggamonga Frog.
You know my custom well:
a riddle, which you must decode,
or hear my dinner bell."

O riddle diddle pie

He asked it in a voice as wild
as fifty chittering birds.
Snickle and wheek! Bubble and squeak!
Not a single sensible word.

O riddle diddle pie

The Riddling Ghost appraised his fork.
"I shall dine well tonight."
"But not on me," the frog exclaimed.
"I challenge you to fight."

O riddle diddle pie

She snatched a big thermometer
embedded in a roast.
Now Froggy had the upper hand,
and now the Riddling Ghost.

O riddle diddle pie

But soon the frog took such a blow
she feared that she would die.
She made a wish and whispered it
under his glittering eye.

O riddle diddle pie

"Brothers and sisters in the swamp,
if you can hear my plea
and you are Chuggamonga Frogs
step up and fight for me."

O riddle diddle pie

A frog appeared and took her place.
The ghost saw nothing strange.
Neither opponent missed a blow,
so swift was the exchange.

O riddle diddle pie

When that one tired, another frog
replaced her unobserved.
The line of frogs crossed twenty swamps.
From pond to pond it curved.

O riddle diddle pie

The Riddling Ghost began to wheeze—
"Let's pause and catch our breath."
Frog number ninety-nine said, "No,
I'll fight you to the death."

O riddle diddle pie

Eight hundred brown frogs later,
the ghost looked tasty and thin.
They popped him in a pastry crust
to keep the flavor in.

O riddle diddle pie

The recipe is secret.
They serve it night and day
at the Moon & Riddles Diner
and the Sunnyside Café.

It's Sweet Potato Day at the Sunnyside Café

I got the special of the day:
the sweet potato pone.
The sun stepped out and threw my dog
a sweet potato bone

and swept night from the corners
with a sweet potato broom.
After I'd fed
on golden bread
he waltzed me to my room.

The master guest-room overlooked
the sweet potato mines.
My comforter was newly stuffed
with sweet potato vines.

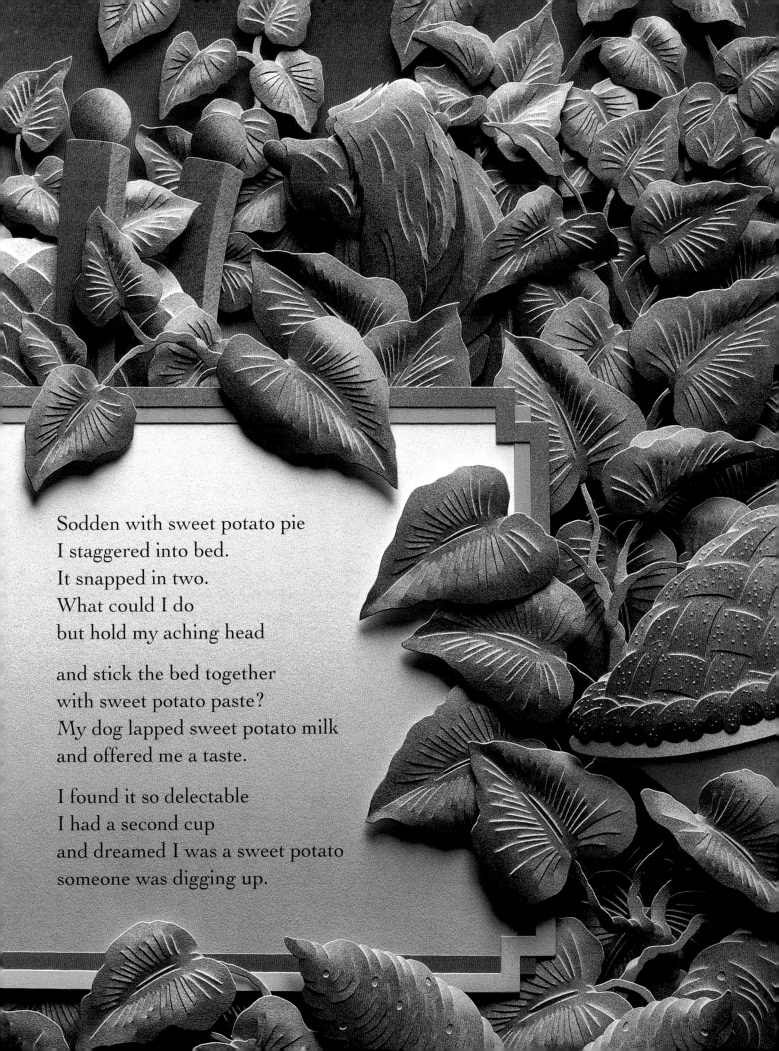

Sodden with sweet potato pie
I staggered into bed.
It snapped in two.
What could I do
but hold my aching head

and stick the bed together
with sweet potato paste?
My dog lapped sweet potato milk
and offered me a taste.

I found it so delectable
I had a second cup
and dreamed I was a sweet potato
someone was digging up.

Dancing All Night

When Shoofly Sally claps her hands
at the Sunnyside Café,
a thousand heifers rock and roll.
They hoof it high,
they hoof it low,
across the Milky Way.

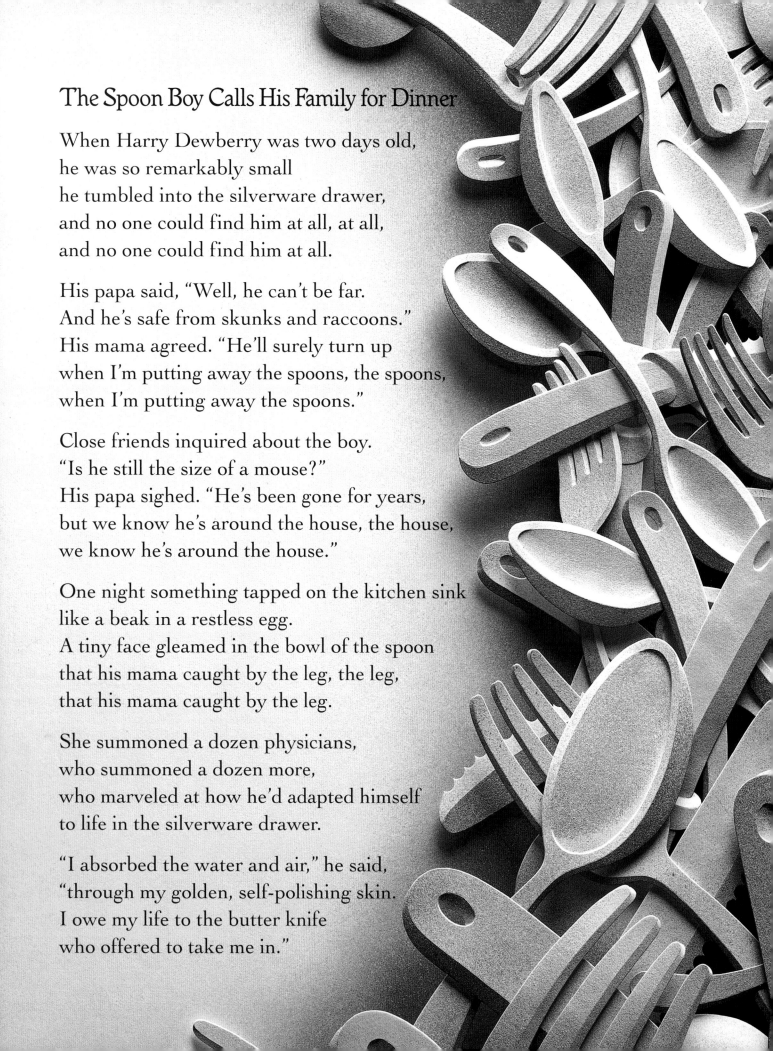

The Spoon Boy Calls His Family for Dinner

When Harry Dewberry was two days old,
he was so remarkably small
he tumbled into the silverware drawer,
and no one could find him at all, at all,
and no one could find him at all.

His papa said, "Well, he can't be far.
And he's safe from skunks and raccoons."
His mama agreed. "He'll surely turn up
when I'm putting away the spoons, the spoons,
when I'm putting away the spoons."

Close friends inquired about the boy.
"Is he still the size of a mouse?"
His papa sighed. "He's been gone for years,
but we know he's around the house, the house,
we know he's around the house."

One night something tapped on the kitchen sink
like a beak in a restless egg.
A tiny face gleamed in the bowl of the spoon
that his mama caught by the leg, the leg,
that his mama caught by the leg.

She summoned a dozen physicians,
who summoned a dozen more,
who marveled at how he'd adapted himself
to life in the silverware drawer.

"I absorbed the water and air," he said,
"through my golden, self-polishing skin.
I owe my life to the butter knife
who offered to take me in."

"I never imagined," his papa exclaimed,
"I'd be asking the spoons to dine.
But the forks are his cousins, not counting the dozens
of uncles in need of a shine, a shine,
of uncles in need of a shine."

When Harry Dewberry clatters to sleep,
he loves for his mother to croon,
The little dog laughed to see such sport,
and the dish ran away with the spoon, the spoon,
and the dish ran away with the spoon.

Shoofly Sally and Her Everything Dog
Clear the Table

"Table for two?" the sun inquired.
We chose a lovely green one.
I slopped my broth on the tablecloth,
and the snow threw down a clean one.

What Shoofly Sally Wrote
with a Cinnamon Stick on the Last Slice of Bread

Let the pample moose grab my galoshes
and the butterflies button my hair.
Tell the Buffalo King when he gives you his ring
that we're going, but no one knows where.

People say that the moon has a dark side
and the sun won't remember my name.
But I'm coming back with a song in my pack,
and I'll sing you to sleep all the same.

Hey diddle diddle, the moon told a riddle,
first to the bread box and then to the bun.
Bow to your partner and strike up the fiddle,
tickle us, pickle us, sweet potato sun.

Recipes from the Moon & Riddles Diner and the Sunnyside Café Cookbook

Recipes created
by Joanne Burlingame

Try these fun and tasty recipes from Shoofly Sally's favorite restaurant. But be sure to have an adult help you cook, because hot ovens and sharp knives can be dangerous.

For Doug Burlingame
and in memory of Mary Burlingame—J. B.

French Toast

Servings: 6

Ingredients:
  2 eggs
  1 tablespoon butter or margarine
  6 slices bread
  Desired topping (suggestions listed below)
Suggested toppings:
  Maple syrup, fresh fruit, jam, confectioner's sugar
Tools:
  A medium-size bowl
  A fork
  A frying pan
  A pancake turner

1. Break the eggs into the bowl.
2. Beat the eggs well with a fork.
3. Place the butter in the frying pan and melt it over medium heat.
4. Dip 1 slice of bread at a time into the beaten eggs, coating both sides.
5. Place the dipped bread in the heated frying pan.
6. Cook until golden, then turn with the pancake turner and cook the other side.
7. Serve immediately with toppings of your choice.

Hoppelpoppel

Servings: 1

Ingredients:
- 1 thin slice salami or boiled ham
  (deli-style)
- 1 egg
- ½ slice American cheese

Tools:
- A greased muffin tin
- A small bowl or coffee cup
- A fork
- A spoon

1. Preheat the oven to 375°.
2. Press the slice of salami (or ham) into
   a greased muffin cup. The slice should
   line the cup, including the sides.
3. Break the egg into the coffee cup or small
   bowl.
4. With the fork, mix the egg well.
5. Break the ½ slice of cheese into small
   pieces and add it to the egg. Mix well.
6. Carefully pour the egg mixture into the
   center of the salami-lined muffin cup.
7. Bake 15 to 20 minutes, or until the egg
   is set.
8. With the spoon, gently remove the
   hoppelpoppel, complete with salami,
   and place on a serving dish.
9. Serve immediately.

You can make a full muffin tin
of hoppelpoppels all at once.

Strawberry Flummery

Servings: 4 to 6

Ingredients:
- 1 3⅜-ounce package instant vanilla
  pudding mix
- 2 cups cold milk
- 1 cup finely chopped strawberries
  (fresh or thawed)
- 1 or 2 sliced strawberries

Tools:
- A medium-size mixing bowl
- A wire whisk
- A wooden spoon
- Plastic wrap

1. Empty the pudding mix into the
   mixing bowl.
2. Add the milk and stir with the wire
   whisk until well blended and smooth.
3. Chill the mixture in the refrigerator
   10 minutes.
4. With the wooden spoon, fold in
   the chopped strawberries.
5. Top with the sliced strawberries.
6. Cover with plastic wrap and chill at least
   1 hour before serving.

Great Bears and Paw Prints

Servings: 2 to 3 dozen

Ingredients:
    1 cup butter, softened
    ½ cup sugar
    2½ cups all-purpose flour
    1 teaspoon vanilla
    Brown food coloring
    Sliced almonds
    Sugar
Tools:
    A large mixing bowl
    An electric mixer
    A rubber spatula
    2 ungreased cookie sheets

1. In the large mixing bowl, combine the butter and ½ cup sugar. Using the electric mixer, mix well.
2. Add the flour and vanilla. Blend well. Use the spatula to scrape the sides of the bowl clean.
3. Add a few drops of the brown food coloring and mix well.
4. Using the dough as if it were clay, make the Great Bear and/or paw prints on each ungreased cookie sheet as shown. Use the sliced almonds for the paw-print nails. The cookies should be ½ inch to 1 inch apart.

5. Sprinkle each cookie with sugar.
6. Place the cookie sheets in the refrigerator and chill about ½ hour.
7. Preheat the oven to 300°.
8. Bake the cookies about 30 minutes, or until set but not browned.
9. Remove from cookie sheets and cool.

Pample Moose Cocktail

Servings: 2

Ingredients:
    1 chilled grapefruit
    2 rounded teaspoons confectioner's sugar
    2 tablespoons desired topping
        (suggestions listed below)
    2 fresh strawberries
Suggested toppings:
    Grenadine, orange juice, raspberry
        syrup, strawberry syrup, honey
Tools:
    2 cereal bowls
    A sharp, thin-bladed knife

1. Cut the chilled grapefruit in half.
2. Place each half of the grapefruit in a bowl.
3. Ask an adult to use the sharp knife to carefully loosen the grapefruit meat from the peel. Remove any seeds and cut away the tough fiber in the center.
4. Sprinkle 1 rounded teaspoon confectioner's sugar on each half of the grapefruit. Let set for 5 minutes.
5. Pour 1 tablespoon topping on each grapefruit half, place a fresh strawberry in the center, and serve immediately.

The Queen of Chickens

Servings: 1

Ingredients:
    2 slices American cheese
    1 leaf iceberg lettuce, shredded
    1 hard-boiled egg (with the shell removed)
    2 ⅛-inch-thick slices carrot

Tools:
    A knife (plastic knife may be used)
    A small plate

1. Stack the slices of cheese and cut as shown, forming bars of cheese.

2. Arrange the cheese bars in the center of the plate, forming a rectangular "box."

3. Place the shredded lettuce in the center of the box to make "hay."
4. Place the hard-boiled egg in the center of the box, on top of the lettuce.
5. With the knife, make 2 small slits in the egg as shown. (Be careful not to slice all the way through.)

6. Cut one of the slices of carrot as shown. The V cuts should be made on the wide curved edge.

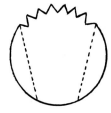

7. Push the narrow end of the carrot into the slit made at the narrow end of the egg. This is the Queen's tail.
8. Cut the second piece of carrot in half. Make V cuts on the curved edge of one of the halves.

9. Push the flat side of the V-cut piece of carrot into the slit made in the wide end of the egg. This is the Queen's comb.
10. From the leftover piece of carrot, cut small pieces and push them into the egg to form the Queen's eyes and beak.
11. Serve immediately.

Everything Dogs

Servings: 4

Ingredients:
  4 hot dogs
  1 8-count tube crescent-roll dough
  Mustard
Tools:
  A knife (plastic knife may be used)
  An ungreased cookie sheet
  A pancake turner

1. Preheat the oven to 375°.
2. Cut 1 hot dog into 2 pieces, as shown. (One is shorter than the other.)

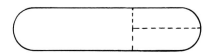

3. Cut the shorter piece of the hot dog in half, lengthwise.
4. Make a slice down the length of the larger piece of hot dog. Be careful not to cut all the way through.

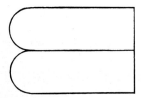

5. Place 1 triangle of dough on the ungreased cookie sheet.
6. Open the larger piece of hot dog and place it, cut side down, on the dough. Fold the dough up and around the hot dog, completely covering it.

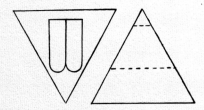

7. Take a second triangle of dough and cut it into 3 pieces, as shown.
8. Wrap the 2 small pieces of hot dog in the larger slices of dough.
9. Place these 2 pieces of hot dog on the cookie sheet on each side of the larger piece of hot dog.
10. Make a ball out of the small piece of dough remaining. Place it on the Everything Dog's face to form his nose.
11. Repeat steps 1 through 10 for the 3 remaining hot dogs.
12. Bake the dogs for 11 to 13 minutes, or until the crescent rolls are golden brown.
13. With mustard, make 2 small dots for eyes on each dog. Use the pancake turner to remove them from the pan. Serve immediately.

Bubble and Squeak

Servings: 4

Ingredients:
- 3 cups cold mashed potatoes
- 1 cup finely chopped cooked cabbage
- 2 tablespoons finely chopped onion (optional)
- 2 tablespoons butter
- 4 slices deli-style roast beef

Tools:
- A medium-size mixing bowl
- A rubber spatula
- A frying pan
- A pancake turner
- A serving platter

1. In the mixing bowl, combine the mashed potatoes, cabbage, and onion (if used). With the rubber spatula, mix well.
2. Melt the butter in the frying pan over medium heat.
3. Quickly brown both sides of the roast beef in the melted butter.
4. With the pancake turner, remove the roast beef and place on a serving platter.
5. Place the potato mixture in the frying pan.
6. Heat the potatoes over medium heat until warm and partially browned.
7. Serve immediately with the warm roast beef.

The Riddling Ghost

Servings: 1

Ingredients:
- 1 slice bread
- Cream cheese
- 2 raisins

Tools:
- A ghost-shaped cookie cutter
- A toaster
- A knife
- A toothpick

1. With the cookie cutter, cut a ghost out of the slice of bread.
2. Lightly toast the ghost. Let it cool.
3. Cover the ghost with cream cheese.
4. Use the raisins to make eyes.
5. With the toothpick, draw a smile on his face.
6. Serve immediately.

The Chuggamonga Frog

Servings: 1

Ingredients:
- 1 large, soft molasses cookie
- 1 scoop lime sherbet (or any flavor green ice cream)
- 2 chocolate chips (or raisins)

Tools:
- A serving dish
- An ice-cream scooper
- A spoon

1. Place the cookie in a serving dish.
2. Top the cookie with the scoop of lime sherbet (or substitute).
3. Push the chips or raisins into the sherbet to make the frog's eyes.
4. With the spoon, make a mouth for the frog.
5. Serve immediately.

Sweet Potato Pone

Servings: 4 to 6

Ingredients:
  3 cups uncooked sweet potatoes
     (peeled, grated, and firmly packed)
  1 teaspoon grated orange peel
  ½ cup orange juice
  2 tablespoons molasses
  2 eggs
  2 tablespoons butter, melted
  ½ teaspoon ground ginger
  ½ teaspoon salt

Tools:
  A grater
  A large mixing bowl
  A wooden spoon
  A greased 1½-quart baking dish with cover

1. Preheat the oven to 350°.
2. Ask an adult to grate the sweet potatoes
   and the orange peel.
3. In the large mixing bowl, combine all the
   ingredients. Mix well with the wooden
   spoon.
4. Pour the batter into the greased baking
   dish.
5. Cover the dish and bake for 20 minutes.
6. Remove the cover and bake the pone
   another 40 minutes, or until the outside
   edges are browned.
7. Serve warm.

Snow Slush

Servings: 1

Ingredients:
  Clean snow (or shaved or crushed ice)
  1 to 3 tablespoons flavored syrup
     (suggestions listed below)

Suggested syrup flavors:
  Maple, grenadine, strawberry,
     raspberry, honey

Tools:
  A coffee cup or mug
  A spoon

1. Gather snow (or ice) in the cup.
2. Pour the desired syrup over the top.
3. Enjoy!

Spoon Bread

Servings: 10 to 12

Ingredients:
- 1½ cups water
- 1 cup cornmeal
- 1 tablespoon sugar
- 1 teaspoon salt
- 1¼ teaspoons baking powder
- 3 tablespoons butter
- 1½ cups milk
- *3 large eggs, separated

Tools:
- A medium-size saucepan
- A wooden spoon
- An egg separator, or a funnel and a small glass
- 2 medium-size mixing bowls (1 for the egg whites)
- A fork
- An electric mixer
- A greased 9-by-13-inch pan
- A serving spoon

1. Preheat the oven to 325°.
2. In the saucepan, bring the water to a rapid boil.
3. Add the cornmeal to the boiling water.
4. Stir constantly with the wooden spoon until the mixture becomes thick and mushy.
5. Remove the pan from the heat.
6. Immediately add the sugar, salt, baking powder, and butter. Blend well using the wooden spoon.
7. Add the milk and mix well.
8. Beat the egg yolks with the fork and add them to the mixture.
9. With the electric mixer, beat the egg whites until they form stiff peaks.
10. Fold the egg whites into the mixture.
11. Pour the batter into the greased pan.
12. Bake 50 to 55 minutes. Serve immediately using the serving spoon.

*If you do not have an egg separator, you can use a funnel and a glass. (Be sure to have a medium-size mixing bowl and coffee cup or small bowl handy for transferring egg whites and yolks.) Place the funnel on top of the glass. Crack the egg open and gently pour it into the funnel. The egg white will fall through to the glass. The yolk will remain in the funnel. If the yolk blocks the funnel opening, gently roll the funnel to release all the egg white. Pour the yolk into the small bowl or cup. Pour the egg white into the mixing bowl. Repeat for the other eggs.

Gypsy Pancakes

Servings: 4

Ingredients:
  1 egg
  *1 cup buttermilk
  2 tablespoons oil
  1 cup all-purpose flour
  1 tablespoon sugar
  1 teaspoon baking powder
  ½ teaspoon baking soda
  ½ teaspoon salt
  Butter
  Maple syrup
Tools:
  A medium-size mixing bowl
  A wire whisk
  A frying pan or griddle
  A spoon
  A pancake turner

1. In the mixing bowl, combine the egg and buttermilk (or substitute), and beat well with the wire whisk.
2. Add the oil, flour, sugar, baking powder, baking soda, and salt, one ingredient at a time. Be sure to beat well after each addition.
3. Preheat the frying pan or griddle. To test if the pan is hot enough, sprinkle the surface of the pan with a few drops of water. If the droplets dance across the pan, the pan is hot enough.
4. With the spoon, drip small amounts of batter in the form of two dots for eyes, a dot for a nose, and a long curved line for a mouth.
5. Allow the facial features to cook until they are covered with bubbles.
6. Gently pour a large circle of batter over and around the facial features.
7. As soon as the pancake is puffed and covered with bubbles, turn the pancake with the pancake turner.
8. Cook the second side of the pancake until it is golden brown.
9. Repeat to make 3 more gypsy pancakes.
10. Serve immediately with butter and maple syrup.

*Buttermilk substitute: In a 1-cup measuring cup, mix 1 tablespoon vinegar and enough whole milk to equal 1 cup.